SEUNG-JU CHOI

김밥

THE KIMBAP COOKBOOK

50+ Delicious and Beginner-Friendly
Recipes for *Rolls, Rice Balls,* and
More *Convenience Store–Style Snacks*

ULYSSES
PRESS

Published in the United States by:
ULYSSES PRESS
PO Box 3440
Berkeley, CA 94703
www.ulyssespress.com

First published in Korea in 2016 as 김밥 · 주먹밥 · 샌드위치 (Gimbap, Rice Balls, and Sandwiches) by LEESCOM Publishing (리스컴)

ISBN: 978-1-64604-715-4
Library of Congress Control Number: 2024934560

Printed in China
10 9 8 7 6 5 4 3 2 1

Photographs: Hae-Won Kim
US editors: Casie Vogel, Claire Chun, Renee Rutledge, Joyce Wu
US front cover and interior design: Winnie Liu

CONTENTS

INTRODUCTION

Want to experience the delicious lunches, snacks, and treats you'd find in a Korean convenience store or lunch box? Look no further than this collection of recipes.

Kimbap is a Korean mainstay found in grocery stores, convenience stores, street stalls, and food markets. These rice balls and rolls are easy to make at home, affordable, and satisfying to eat in one bite. They're delicious, nutritious, and perfect for a quick snack, lunch box, or picnic.

Some kimbap favorites combine fresh fish, various vegetables, fruits, and cheese. Don't be scared to make your own kimbap. You can whip them up quickly with ingredients you always have in the refrigerator, without having to shop separately. Kimbap is versatile and allows you to get creative by simply changing ingredients like eggs, seaweed, beef, anchovies, squid, or tuna.

Many people still think making rolls is difficult, so they don't try making them at home. However, rolls are actually easy and simple to make. From your home kitchen, try making California rolls that melt in your mouth. There's nothing better than a light and refreshing meal or a neat and heartfelt lunch box.

Sandwiches are another popular treat made with soft and savory bread filled with fresh and nutritious ingredients. Korean sandwiches are often inspired by Western classics like hamburgers and hot dogs, but also bring their own unique flavors by adding layers of mashed potatoes between soft, fluffy sandwich bread.

How to Use This Book

The ingredients listed in this book are based on serving four people. If you're making two servings, you only need to prepare half of the main ingredients, and for seasonings, add a bit more than half, but don't add them all at once. Sprinkle them in gradually while tasting to avoid mistakes.

In directions for each recipe, detailed explanations are provided for handling ingredients and cooking processes so that even beginners can easily follow along. If any part is unclear, refer to the step-by-step photos.

Furthermore, in sections called "Basic Techniques," additional how-to's include everything from cooking and seasoning rice to mixing vinegar sauce to shaping sushi and rice balls.

BASIC TECHNIQUES

HOW TO MAKE TASTY KIMBAP

Make the Seasoned Rice

Prep your rice. Rinse the rice thoroughly and drain to remove excess water. Let it sit for about 1 hour to allow the grains to swell evenly. Do not use sticky or glutinous rice, as it can make the kimbap difficult to roll.

Use less water than usual. Cook the rice with ¼ to ⅓ less water than you usually use. Adding a few drops of rice wine (cheongju) to the rice and water combination gives the grains elasticity and a glossy appearance.

Add a vinegar mixture. While you wait for your rice to cook, create a vinegar mixture to season your rice. This one works for 4 cups of freshly cooked rice. In a small saucepan over low heat, combine 2 tablespoons of rice vinegar, 1 tablespoon of sugar, and a pinch of salt (about ½ teaspoon). Mix until the sugar dissolves completely. Remove from the heat and mix into your rice.

Cool the rice completely. Make sure your rice cools completely before making kimbap. Heat and steam make seaweed soggy.

Prep Other Ingredients

Use lightly toasted seaweed. Using seaweed without toasting might result in a distinct fishy flavor and could make it soggy more easily. You can toast the seaweed yourself in a heated pan or, more conveniently, buy preroasted seaweed sheets at the supermarket.

Squeeze the Korean pickled radish (danmuji). Before using the pickled radish, rinse it in water and squeeze it hard. If you use pickled radish without draining it, you will add too much extra moisture to your kimbap.

Add some greens, either cucumber or spinach. If you want a crisp and refreshing taste, use cucumber. Slice cucumbers thick and long, then pickle them in a mixture of vinegar and sugar. If you prefer a nutty and firm texture, use spinach. Blanch the leaves, then season them with sesame oil and salt. Do not add minced garlic to kimbap-style spinach because it has too strong a flavor.

Prep your carrots according to preference. Carrots can be sliced long like cucumbers, then blanched in boiling water, or finely julienned and stir-fried in vegetable oil.

Create egg strips. Crack eggs into a fine sieve to break up the yolk before cooking them in a square pan until cooked through; cool and cut into thick strips. If too much oil is used, bubbles may form in the egg strips and they may break apart.

Lightly sauté sliced ham. Cut ham into kimbap-size strips and briefly sauté them in a lightly oiled pan and cool before adding to kimbap.

Divide crab sticks (imitation crab). Use a knife to cleanly cut crab sticks in half for use. However, since crab sticks can easily spoil, it's best not to include them in outdoor summer lunches.

Tips for Making Pretty Rolls

Pay attention to the order of ingredients not only for a visually appealing mix of colors, but also to make sure ingredients do not fall out. Ingredients like julienned carrots, burdock roots, meat, etc., which are prone to scatter easily, should be neatly arranged at the bottom, while thicker ingredients should be placed on top. Otherwise, when rolling, the julienned ingredients may spill or scatter easily.

Use a bamboo rolling mat to ensure uniform thickness and neatness. A tightly woven bamboo mat is preferable; this is also known as a sushi mat. When making inside-out rolls, cover the mat with plastic wrap to help keep the rice from sticking to the mat.

Let the kimbap roll sit for 5 to 10 minutes before slicing. If you slice it immediately after rolling, the seaweed may be too crispy, leading to tearing or unraveling of the ends.

Clean the knife blade with cold water as you slice. When slicing kimbap, rice grains can stick to the knife blade and make it difficult to slice cleanly. Wiping the blade with a cloth dampened in cold water or lemon juice ensures a smooth cut.

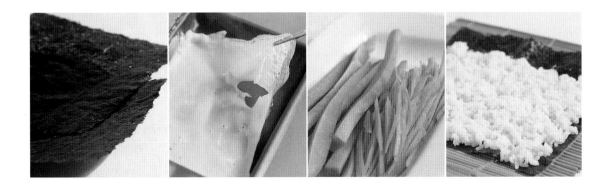

Part 1 Kimbap

Kimbap is great for picnics, work lunches, or tasty on-the-go snacks for children and adults alike. Cucumber, carrots, Korean pickled radish, ham, burdock, beef, crab sticks, tuna, eel, fish eggs, and various other foods can be used. These nutrient-packed rolls can be a healthy and easy meal.

Tuna Kimbap

The tuna, mayonnaise, and
mustard mixture of Tuna Kimbap
is smooth but savory.

Ingredients

4 cups seasoned rice (see page 3)

2 tablespoons black sesame seeds

2 (5-ounce) cans tuna, drained

3 tablespoons mayonnaise

2 tablespoons Dijon mustard

3 tablespoons minced yellow onions

pinch of salt

black pepper, to taste

4 crab sticks

4 sheets roasted seaweed

4 pieces Korean pickled daikon radish (danmuji)

Directions

1. In a large bowl, mix the seasoned rice and black sesame seeds until combined.

2. In a medium bowl, mash the tuna with a spoon. Mix in the mayonnaise, mustard, minced onion, salt, and black pepper.

3. Cut the crab sticks lengthwise into three even pieces, and tear into thinner pieces with your fingers.

4. To roll the kimbap, place the roasted seaweed on a bamboo rolling mat and spread the seasoned rice on two-thirds of the seaweed. Then add the pickled radishes, crab pieces, and tuna on top of the rice, and roll. Repeat with the remaining seaweed sheets and ingredients.

5. Let sit for 5 to 10 minutes then cut each roll into ¾-inch-thick pieces.

1   2   3   4

Egg Roll Kimbap

Try something new by rolling your kimbap with jidan (egg garnish). Not only is it delicious, but the bright yellow adds a nice pop of color. It's a popular lunch option for kids to take to school!

Ingredients

slight drizzle of cooking oil

2 fishcake squares

4 pieces Korean pickled radish

1 medium carrot

⅔ medium cucumber

4 sheets roasted seaweed

4 cups seasoned rice (see page 3)

Jidan (Egg Garnish)

8 eggs

splash of sweet cooking wine

pinch of salt

Fishcake Seasoning

1 tablespoon soy sauce

splash of neutral oil

splash of sesame oil

minced fresh garlic, to taste

splash of corn syrup

Pickling Brine

1 tablespoon sugar

1 tablespoon rice or white wine vinegar

Directions

1. To make the jidan, crack the eggs in a medium bowl. Add the cooking wine and pinch of salt and mix well. Very lightly grease a large pan over medium-high heat. Pour a portion of the egg mixture into the pan and swirl the pan to quickly spread the mixture into a thin, even layer. When it's fully cooked, remove and let cool. Repeat this process to make 6 sheets of jidan. Once the jidan sheets are cooled, cut them into squares roughly the same size as the seaweed.

2. Combine the the pickling brine ingredients in a small bowl.

3. Cut the carrot and cucumber about the same size as the pickled radish and put them in the pickling brine. After an hour, squeeze out the excess brine.

4. Cut the fishcake about the same size as the pickled radish, then lightly stir-fry with the fishcake seasoning.

5. Squeeze out any excess moisture from the pickled radish.

6. To roll the kimbap, place a sheet of jidan on a bamboo rolling mat wrapped in plastic wrap. Put the roasted seaweed on top. Spread the seasoned rice on the seaweed. Add some fishcake, carrots, cucumbers, and pickled radish then roll. Repeat with the remaining ingredients.

7. Let sit for 5 to 10 minutes then cut each roll into 1-inch-thick pieces.

Anchovy Kimbap

If you can handle spice, you will
love the anchovies mixed with spicy
Cheongyang chili peppers.

Ingredients

½ cup small anchovies

4 Cheongyang chili peppers, deseeded and finely chopped

1 tablespoon rice wine (cheongju)

pinch of salt

4 cups seasoned rice (see page 3)

4 long slices of seasoned burdock root

4 long pieces of fishcake

4 sheets roasted seaweed

Anchovy Seasoning

2 tablespoons cooking oil

2 tablespoons soy sauce

2 teaspoons corn syrup

2 teaspoons minced fresh garlic

Fishcake Seasoning

2 teaspoons cooking oil

2 teaspoons soy sauce

½ teaspoon minced garlic

½ teaspoon sugar

pinch of salt

Directions

1. Put the dried anchovies in a colander and wash under running water. When done, remove as much water as you can.

2. In a heated frying pan over medium-high heat, add the anchovy seasoning. When the edges of the sauce start to simmer, add the prepared anchovies, Cheongyang peppers, rice wine, and a pinch of salt then stir-fry until the peppers are soft.

3. In another heated frying pan, add the fishcake with the fishcake seasoning and stir-fry for about 2 minutes.

4. To roll the kimbap, place the seaweed onto a bamboo rolling mat. Spread the seasoned rice on the seaweed. Add some anchovies, a piece of fishcake, and a piece of burdock and roll. Repeat with the remaining seaweed sheets and ingredients.

5. Let sit for 5 to 10 minutes then cut each roll into 1-inch-thick pieces.

Squid Kimbap

Seasoning squid with gochujang creates the perfect combination of spicy and savory. And it's even better when you add in sesame leaves!

Ingredients

1 medium squid

1 tablespoon neutral cooking oil

12 perilla (sesame) leaves, trimmed

¼ cup alfalfa sprouts, trimmed

4 sheets roasted seaweed

4 cups seasoned rice (see page 3)

Squid Seasoning

1½ tablespoons gochujang (fermented red chili pepper paste)

2 teaspoons sesame oil

1 teaspoon minced fresh garlic

1 teaspoon sugar

½ teaspoon soy sauce

pinch of salt

pinch of black pepper powder

Directions

1. To prepare the squid, cut the legs off the squid and dice the body. In a medium bowl, mix the squid parts with the squid seasoning until evenly coated.

2. Coat the frying pan in the tablespoon of oil and add in the seasoned squid. Stir-fry until no visible liquid remains.

3. Rinse the perilla leaves and alfalfa sprouts then strain out any excess water.

4. To roll the kimbap, place the seaweed onto a bamboo rolling mat. Spread the seasoned rice on the seaweed. Place 2 or 3 perilla leaves over the rice before adding the stir-fried squid and alfalfa sprouts. Repeat with the remaining seaweed sheets and ingredients.

5. Let sit for 5 to 10 minutes then cut each roll into 1-inch-thick pieces.

Eel Kimbap

Eel is an excellent source of protein, so this makes the perfect lunch to get you through a work or school day! The secret to this tasty kimbap is the eel sauce, so make sure you follow the recipe to a T.

Ingredients

2 eels, halved

1 knob ginger, peeled and julienned

4 cups seasoned rice (see page 3)

2 sheets roasted seaweed, cut into ½-inch-thick strips

Eel Sauce

½ knob ginger, minced

3 cloves garlic, minced

½ green onion, cut into thick pieces

4 tablespoons soy sauce

1 tablespoon corn syrup

1 tablespoon rice wine (cheongju)

1 teaspoon sesame oil

pinch of salt

black pepper powder, to taste

Directions

1. Steam the eel in a pot for 5 minutes. Doing so will help the sauce absorb into the eel.

2. In a large bowl, mix the ginger, garlic, and green onion with the remaining eel sauce ingredients. Pour the sauce into a pan and let simmer.

3. Place the steamed eel in the sauce on the pan until it is thoroughly soaked, then turn the eel over. When the eel is cooked all the way through and the sauce is completely absorbed, remove the eel and cut it into 1-inch-thick pieces.

4. Soak the julienned ginger in water for several minutes to get rid of the bitterness.

5. Shape the seasoned rice into bite-size pieces.

6. To finish the kimbap, place 1 piece of eel on each rice ball and top it off with chopped ginger pieces. Wrap a strip of seaweed around the rice. Repeat with the remaining ingredients.

3   4   5

Kimchi Pork Roll

This is a great snack to make if you're looking to use up the kimchi in your fridge. The more sour, the better!

Ingredients

½ pound pork, cut into small pieces

⅓ yellow onion, thinly sliced

½ head kimchi cabbage

2 tablespoons sesame oil

4 cups seasoned rice (see page 3)

Pork Marinade

1 tablespoon soy sauce

2 teaspoons ginger juice

1 teaspoon minced fresh garlic

1 tablespoon sesame oil

pinch of salt

black pepper powder, to taste

Directions

1. To make the pork bulgogi, add the pork pieces and marinade ingredients in a large bowl, and let sit for about 30 minutes.

2. In a frying pan over medium to high heat, add the seasoned pork and onion and stir until the moisture is gone.

3. Cut off the thick stems of the cabbage kimchi and use only the thin wide leaves. Rinse thoroughly in water. Squeeze out any excess liquid and season the kimchi leaves with sesame oil.

4. To wrap the kimbap, spread out the cabbage leaves on a cutting board. Place a bite-size amount of rice on top of each cabbage leaf. Add the pork bulgogi on top of the rice and roll. Repeat with the remaining ingredients.

2 3 4

Beef Roll

Not every roll has to have seaweed!
Instead, try using thin slices of beef.

Ingredients

¾ pound beef tenderloin

2 tablespoons neutral oil

1 medium carrot, cut into long strips

pinch of salt, plus more to taste

½ bunch spinach

sesame oil, to taste

4 cups seasoned rice (see page 3)

Beef Marinade

3 tablespoons soy sauce

1 tablespoon sesame oil

2 tablespoons rice wine (cheongju)

½ tablespoon salt

2 cloves garlic

1 dry red chile pepper

⅔ cup water

pinch of salt

black pepper powder, to taste

Directions

1. Cut the beef tenderloin to the size of your palm and place it on a cutting board, then pound it with a meat mallet. If you don't have a meat mallet, use the back of a knife, the bottom of a saucepan, or a rolling pin.

2. Add all the ingredients for the beef marinade to a large pot and bring to a gentle boil. Once the marinade is heated through, add the beef, flipping it continuously until fully cooked.

3. Heat the oil in a pan over low to medium heat and stir-fry the carrots. Season with a pinch of salt.

4. In a separate pot, blanch the spinach for 1 minute in boiling water. Drain in a colander and rinse in cold water. Squeeze out any excess water and add to a medium bowl. Add sesame oil and salt for flavor.

5. To roll the kimbap, place the marinated beef on a bamboo rolling mat and spread the seasoned rice evenly on the beef. Place the carrots and spinach on top of the rice and roll. Repeat with the remaining ingredients.

6. Cut each roll into ½-inch-thick pieces.

Chungmu Kimbap

Chungmu Kimbap, a roll originating
from the southern coastal region
of Korea, satisfies your craving
for rice and seaweed. It pairs well
with spicy radish and squid salad.

Ingredients

⅓ Korean daikon radish, peeled and cut into ⅓-inch cubes

2 whole squid, cut into ⅓-inch cubes

4 sheets roasted seaweed

4 cups seasoned rice (see page 3)

Radish Seasoning

pinch of salt

2 tablespoons sugar

2 tablespoons rice or white wine vinegar

1½ tablespoons gochugaru (Korean red chili powder)

2 teaspoons minced fresh garlic

Squid Seasoning

1 tablespoon gochugaru

1½ tablespoons soy sauce

2 teaspoons minced fresh garlic

1 tablespoon sesame oil

½ tablespoon rice wine (cheongju)

2 tablespoons neutral oil

Directions

1. In a large bowl, pickle the radish cubes in the salt, sugar, and vinegar, about 2 hours. Drain the radish, then season with the gochugaru and minced garlic.

2. Combine the squid with the squid seasoning in a large bowl. Stir-fry in a large pan until just done; do not overcook.

3. Cut the seaweed sheets into 6 pieces. Add one spoonful of rice on each piece of seaweed and roll.

4. Put the kimbap rolls, squid, and seasoned radish on a plate and serve.

Pork Cutlet Kimbap

Craving something deep fried? The crispy pork cutlet in this roll is perfect.

Ingredients

3½ ounces pork tenderloin, cut into strips

1 cup neutral cooking oil

4 baby dill pickles, cut into strips

4 sheets roasted seaweed

4 tablespoons mayonnaise

4 cups seasoned rice (see page 3)

Pork Seasoning

2 tablespoons onion juice

1 tablespoon rice wine (cheongju)

pinch of salt

black pepper powder, to taste

Cutlet Batter

¼ cup flour

1 egg

½ cup breadcrumbs

Directions

1. In a large bowl, marinate the pork in the pork seasoning for at least 30 minutes.

2. Prepare the cutlet batter ingredients. Spread the flour and breadcrumbs onto individual plates. Crack the egg into a small bowl and scramble.

3. After marinating the pork, take a strip and coat it in flour, covering it on all sides. Dip the pork into the eggs then place it into the breadcrumbs. Flip it to make sure all of the strip is covered in the mixture. Repeat this for each piece. Add the oil to a skillet over medium heat. Fry the pork until golden brown and cooked.

4. To roll the kimbap, place 1 strip of seaweed onto a bamboo rolling mat and spread rice on ⅔ of the seaweed. Spread 1 tablespoon of mayonnaise on the rice before placing the pork cutlet and dill pickles on top then roll. Repeat with the remaining seaweed sheets and ingredients.

5. Let sit for 5 to 10 minutes then cut each roll into ½-inch-thick pieces.

Mayak Kimbap

Mayak kimbap originated in the Gwangjang Market, one of the best places to go for Korean street food in Seoul. This kimbap is named "mayak," the Korean word for "drug," because it is addictive!

Ingredients

1 cucumber, peeled and roughly julienned into 2-inch-long pieces

1 medium carrot, chopped into 2-inch-long pieces

salt, to taste

6 sheets roasted seaweed

4 cups seasoned rice (see page 3)

½ Korean pickled radish, chopped into 2-inch-long pieces

Pickle Brine

2 tablespoons rice or white wine vinegar

1 tablespoon salt

1 tablespoon sugar

Mustard Sauce

2 tablespoons soy sauce

1 tablespoon Korean hot mustard (gyeoja)

1 tablespoon white vinegar

1 tablespoon water

2 teaspoon sugar

Directions

1. In a small bowl, combine the cucumber with the pickle brine. Pickle for about 30 minutes, then squeeze out any excess liquid.

2. Add the carrots in a light and even layer to a frying pan and stir-fry. Add salt to taste.

3. Cut each seaweed sheet into 4 even squares.

4. Spread the seasoned rice on a seaweed square. Put some pickled radish, carrots, and cucumbers on top of the rice and roll. Repeat with the remaining ingredients.

5. In a small bowl, mix the mustard sauce ingredients to make a dip for the kimbap.

3   4

Stir-Fried Beef Samgak Kimbap

This popular triangle-shaped kimbap is usually sold in Korean convenience stores but you can now make your own at home! Instead of kimchi and bulgogi, you can use tuna, crab, and vegetables.

Ingredients

¼ pound beef, finely chopped

1 tablespoon sesame oil

1 triangle rice ball (onigiri) mold

4 cups seasoned rice (see page 3)

3 stems cabbage kimchi, finely chopped

8 sheets roasted seaweed, halved

Beef Seasoning

2 tablespoons soy sauce

2 tablespoons minced onion

2 tablespoons sesame oil

1 teaspoon minced fresh garlic

1 teaspoon sugar

½ teaspoon rice wine (cheongju)

pinch of salt

black pepper powder, to taste

Directions

1. Combine all the beef seasoning ingredients in a bowl. Add the chopped beef and marinate for at least 15 to 30 minutes, or up to 2 hours in the refrigerator.

2. In a medium pan on medium-high heat, stir-fry the beef in the sesame oil until cooked.

3. Fill half of the mold with rice. Add the kimchi and bulgogi and cover with more rice. Gently press the mold lid down on the rice then remove the rice ball from the mold. You now have a triangular kimbap.

4. Place each kimbap at the top of a seaweed sheet half. Fold the bottom half of the sheet up and over the kimbap so it comes just to the top of the rice. Press the seaweed against the side of the triangle to make sure it sticks. Flip the triangle over and press the seaweed onto the back side of the triangle. If needed, use a little water to help the seaweed sheets stick together. Repeat with the remaining seaweed sheets and ingredients.

Flying Fish Roe Kimbap

The vibrant color of flying fish roe makes it the perfect garnish for kimbap. But it is also fun to eat because it pops in your mouth like bubbles when you chew on it.

Ingredients

1 cucumber, cut into strips

4 pieces burdock root, peeled and cut into strips the length and thickness of a chopstick

sprinkle of vinegar

1 cup flying fish roe

3½ ounces mozzarella, cut into strips

pinch of salt

4 sheets roasted seaweed

4 cups seasoned rice (see page 3)

Burdock Seasoning

1 tablespoon soy sauce

1 tablespoon sugar

splash of rice wine (cheongju)

Directions

1. Sprinkle the cucumber with a little salt and let sit for 10 to 15 minutes. Pat dry with a paper towel to remove excess moisture.

2. In a pot of boiling water, add a sprinkle of vinegar and blanch the burdock about 2 minutes or to desired tenderness. In a saucepan on medium heat, simmer the blanched burdock with the burdock seasoning until reduced and shiny, 7 to 8 minutes.

3. Use a strainer to wash the flying fish roe in cold water. Strain any excess water.

4. Cut the seaweed sheets to the size of the sushi mat.

5. To roll the kimbap, place a seaweed sheet on a mat wrapped in plastic wrap. Spread a layer of the rice evenly over the sheet. Sprinkle the flying fish roe evenly on the rice then firmly press into the rice. Flip the sheet over so that the rice is on the bottom and the seaweed is on the top.

6. Place the mozarella, cucumber, and marinated burdock on the seaweed and very carefully roll so that the flying fish roe won't fall off. Repeat with the remaining seaweed sheets and ingredients.

Salad Kimbap

The colorful carrots, cucumbers, cabbage, and bell peppers make this kimbap a fun snack to make when you have company over!

Ingredients

⅓ carrot, diced to the size of a corn kernel

⅔ cucumber, diced to the size of a corn kernel

½ yellow bell pepper, diced to the size of a corn kernel

2 red cabbage leaves, diced to the size of a corn kernel

coarse salt, to taste

5 tablespoons mayonnaise

3 tablespoons chopped peanuts

4 cups seasoned rice (see page 3)

6 sheets roasted seaweed, cut into 1- to 1 ½-inch-thick pieces

½ beet, finely sliced, to garnish

Directions

1. Sprinkle the vegetables with the coarse salt and let sit for 10 to 15 minutes. Wrap the salted vegetables with dry gauze or paper towels then squeeze lightly to drain any excess liquid.

2. In a medium bowl, mix the vegetables and the finely chopped peanuts with mayonnaise to make the salad.

3. With your hands, mold a small handful of rice into a rice ball. Wrap a piece of seaweed around each rice ball, leaving a space above each ball for the salad.

4. Add the salad to the kimbap. Garnish with beets on top. Repeat with the remaining ingredeints.

Avocado Kimbap

Dip this cone-shaped kimbap in a
mustard-based soy sauce that gives
a little kick to your taste buds.

Ingredients

1 avocado, halved, pitted, peeled, and thinly sliced

pinch of salt

black pepper powder, to taste

6 sheets roasted seaweed, quartered

4 cups seasoned rice (see page 3)

6 sticks Korean pickled radish

1 pack radish sprouts

Mustard Soy Sauce

½ tablespoon Korean hot mustard (gyeoja)

3 tablespoons soy sauce

1 tablespoon white vinegar

Directions

1. Sprinkle a pinch of salt and black pepper powder onto the avocado.

2. Put 2 tablespoons of rice on the end of 1 seaweed sheet. Place 1 slice of avocado, 1 radish stick, and a bit of radish sprouts next to the rice and roll into a cone shape. Repeat to make the rest of your kimbap.

3. In a small bowl, combine the mustard sauce ingredients. Serve as a dipping sauce for the kimbap.

Burdock Beef Kimbap

Once you've experienced the crunchy burdock root combined with flavorful beef, you won't want to make any other meal except this classic kimbap.

Ingredients

sprinkle of vinegar

4 pieces burdock root, peeled and cut into strips the length and thickness of a chopstick

¼ pound beef, finely chopped

2 tablespoons neutral oil, divided

1 medium carrot, cut into long strips

pinch of salt, plus more to taste

½ bunch spinach

sesame oil, to taste

4 pieces Korean pickled radish

4 sheets roasted seaweed

4 cups seasoned rice (see page 3)

Jidan (Egg Garnish)

4 eggs

splash of sweet cooking wine

pinch of salt

neutral oil, to grease pan

Directions

1. To a pot of boiling water, add a sprinkle of vinegar and blanch the burdock, about 2 minutes or to desired tenderness. In a saucepan on medium heat, simmer the blanched burdock with the burdock seasoning until reduced and shiny, 7 to 8 minutes.

2. In a large bowl, marinate the beef with the seasoning ingredients, then evenly coat a frying pan with a tablespoon of neutral oil and stir-fry the meat until cooked.

3. Heat another tablespoon of neutral oil in a pan over low to medium heat and stir-fry the carrots. Season with a pinch of salt.

4. In a separate pot, blanch the spinach for 1 minute in boiling water. Drain in a colander and rinse in cold water. Squeeze out any excess water and transfer to a medium bowl. Add sesame oil and salt for flavor.

5. To make the jidan, crack the eggs in a medium bowl. Add the cooking wine and pinch of salt and mix well. Very lightly grease a large pan over medium-high heat. Pour the egg mixture into the pan and swirl the pan to quickly spread the mixture into a thin, even layer. When it's cooked, remove and let cool, then cut lengthwise into ½-inch-thick pieces.

Beef Seasoning

1 tablespoon soy sauce

a few drops of sesame oil

sugar, to taste

minced fresh garlic, to taste

Burdock Seasoning

1 tablespoon soy sauce

1 tablespoon sugar

rice wine (cheongju), to taste

1 tablespoon soy sauce

a few drops of sesame oil

sugar, to taste

minced fresh garlic, to taste

6. To roll the kimbap, place a seaweed sheet onto a bamboo rolling mat. Spread the seasoned rice on the seaweed. Place the beef, burdock, carrots, spinach, pickled radish, and jidan on top of the rice and roll. Repeat with the remaining ingredients.

1   2   4   5

BASIC TECHNIQUES

MAKING FRESH AND DELICIOUS SUSHI AT HOME

Making sushi at home might seem challenging, but it's actually quite simple once you know how to cook rice and handle basic ingredients. Why not give it a try and feel like a chef for a change?

Mixing Sushi Vinegar

As with kimbap, sushi rice is seasoned with a vinegar mixture (see page 3 for a recipe). Sushi vinegar enhances the taste but also prevents rice in sushi from spoiling easily. The ideal ratio for sushi vinegar is 2 parts rice vinegar to 1 part sugar, with salt added to taste. The ratio of sushi vinegar to rice is about ½ tablespoon of sushi vinegar for each cup of rice.

Shaping Sushi Rice

Scoop a suitable amount of rice with one hand and place it on the palm of the other hand. Then, use the other hand to gently shape it into a slightly elongated shape for bite-size sushi. Avoid pressing too hard, as it will make the rice too firm and lose its flavor. Using a mold can help you easily shape the rice.

To prevent the rice grains from sticking to your hands when forming the rice balls, dip your hands in lemon water. Wetting your hands frequently while working with rice is key to prevent sticking. Using plain water might dilute the sushi vinegar flavor, so add lemon juice to the water or place thick slices of lemon in the water.

Adding Flavor

If you'd like, spread a moderate amount of spicy mustard on the bite-size rice balls. Avoid adding too much mustard, as it may overpower the taste of the ingredients.

Dip the mustard-coated rice balls in soy sauce with a squeeze of lemon juice for an exquisite taste. Mustard soy sauce complements not only raw fish sushi but also hand rolls with avocado, vegetables, and kimchi.

Types of Sushi Fish

At some supermarkets, you may find pre-packaged slices of raw fish specifically for sushi. If you're not confident in handling raw fish yourself, buying these pre-packaged slices makes it very easy to make sushi at home. Otherwise, you can ask the staff at the fish section of department stores or supermarkets to slice fresh fish thickly for you. However, since freshness is crucial for raw fish, it's best to use it immediately after purchase. Just make sure you use sushi-grade fish if you plan to eat it raw.

Salmon is one of the most popular sushi ingredients due to its translucent pink hue, smooth texture, and rich flavor.

Scallop is known for its tender texture.

Tuna sushi is made from the red-flesh part of tuna. Unlike the white flesh, the red flesh is lean, making its taste clean and pure.

Crab sushi is made from crab leg meat. It has a sweet and savory taste.

Flatfish, also known as hirame or Japanese turbot, is widely used in sushi because of its clean and refreshing taste.

Avocado tastes savory, similar to butter. When you make sushi with avocado, it brings out the flavor of other ingredients.

Egg roll, or tamago, is made from cooked scrambled eggs cut into squares. It can be placed on sushi.

Cockle has a dark brown color and is sold in stores after being cleaned and blanched.

Shrimp has a unique sweet flavor. After blanching and peeling raw shrimp, split it in half before using.

Octopus legs are blanched and thinly sliced. They have a chewy texture that is enjoyable.

Hanchi (cuttlefish) is similar to squid but with a mild taste and tender texture. It can be eaten raw.

Surf clam, or hokkigai, has a chewy texture and excellent flavor.

So much flavor!

Part 2 **Rice Balls**

Easy to make and easy to eat, rice balls are a delicious meal or anytime snack. Get creative and mix in your favorite ingredients or leftover side dishes! Perfect for busy mornings when you don't have a lot of time to pack a lunch or snack, these can be thrown into your bag or school lunches for a tasty meal.

Beef Rice Balls

Marinated and chopped beef is stir-fried with rice to make a salty, seasoned, and one-of-a-kind rice ball.

Ingredients

⅓ pound beef, trimmed and finely chopped

1 tablespoon neutral oil

4 cups cooked rice

2 green onions, thinly sliced

lettuce leaves (optional)

Beef Marinade

1½ tablespoons soy sauce

2 teaspoons sugar

½ tablespoon sesame oil

1 teaspoon rice wine (cheongju)

pinch of salt

black pepper, to taste

Directions

1. Combine all the beef marinade ingredients in a bowl. Add the chopped beef and marinate for at least 15 to 30 minutes, or up to 2 hours in the refrigerator.

2. Heat a medium frying pan to medium-high heat. Remove the beef from the marinade and stir-fry until any liquid evaporates and the beef is browned.

3. Once the beef is cooked, add the rice to the pan with the tablespoon of oil. Mix well and stir-fry for a minute until heated through.

4. Let the beef and rice mixture cool slightly, then shape it into round balls with your hands.

5. Place each rice ball into baking cups and garnish with thinly sliced green onions. You can also wrap them individually with lettuce leaves for packing in lunch boxes.

1

2

3

4

Bibim Rice Balls

These misshappen rice balls may be ugly to some, but they are above all delicious. Improvise with the ingredients and use items you have left over at home.

Ingredients

2 sheets roasted seaweed

4 cups warm rice

2 tablespoons furikake

3 tablespoons sesame seeds

4 crab sticks, sliced thick

2 green onions, green parts only, thinly sliced

1 tablespoon sesame oil

salt, to taste

Directions

1. Put the toasted seaweed in a plastic bag then crush into small pieces.

2. In a large bowl, combine the freshly cooked rice, crushed seaweed, furikake, sesame seeds, crab sticks, and green onions. Mix thoroughly.

3. Add the sesame oil and salt to the rice mixture. Combine and add more oil or salt to taste.

4. Shape the rice mixture into bite-size balls, then skewer individually on toothpicks or skewers. Place neatly in a lunch box or on a plate.

1   2   3   4

Seaweed Rice Balls

Even those who think they don't enjoy seaweed will love this simple but delectable combo of seaweed, rice, and sesame oil.

Ingredients

5 sheets roasted seaweed

4 cups warm rice

¼ red bell pepper, diced

2 tablespoons neutral oil

1 tablespoon sesame oil

pinch of salt

sprinkle of sesame seeds

Seaweed Seasoning

2 tablespoons soy sauce

1 tablespoon sesame oil

1 tablespoon finely chopped green onions

½ tablespoon sesame seeds

2 teaspoons sugar

2 tablespoons water

Directions

1. Tear seaweed sheets into small flakes. To avoid scattering the flakes, you can put the seaweed in a plastic bag and simply tear or break by hand while it's in the bag.

2. In a large bowl, combine all the ingredients for the seaweed seasoning. Mix well.

3. Add the seaweed flakes into the bowl with the seaweed seasoning. Mix until the seaweed flakes are evenly coated.

4. Add the remaining ingredients to the bowl and mix thoroughly.

5. Once the rice and seaweed mixture is well combined, let it cool slightly. Shape it into bite-size rice balls and serve.

Banded Rice Balls

Wrapped in bands made with red crab meat, yellow eggs, and green vegetables, these rice balls delight with their beautiful colors and shape.

Ingredients

2 eggs

handful of mitsuba (Japanese parsley) or celery leaves, stems trimmed

salt, to taste

5 crab sticks, halved lengthwise

6 sticks Korean pickled radish, cut in 1½- to 2-inch slices

4 cups seasoned rice (see page 3)

Egg Garnish Seasoning

½ tablespoon rice wine (cheongju)

2 teaspoons sweet cooking wine

salt, to taste

Pickled Radish Seasoning

2 tablespoons sugar

2 tablespoons rice vinegar

Mustard Soy Sauce

2 tablespoons soy sauce

2 teaspoons Korean hot mustard (gyeoja)

Directions

1. In a large bowl, beat the eggs with the egg garnish seasoning. In a heated pan, pour half the egg mixture into a thin layer. Cook until the egg sets, then flip and cook briefly on the other side. Repeat with the remaining egg mixture. Once cooked, remove from the pan and slice into thin strips.

2. Fill a medium pot with water and bring to a boil over high heat. Blanch the mitsuba or celery leaves in the boiling water for about 30 seconds. Remove from the pot and immediately transfer to a bowl of ice water to stop the cooking process. Once cooled, drain the mitsuba and squeeze out any excess water. Lightly season with salt.

3. In a small bowl, combine the ingredients for the radish seasoning and add the radish.

4. With slightly damp hands to prevent sticking, take a handful of seasoned rice and shape into a ball.

5. Place a strip of pickled radish in the center of the rice ball. Wrap the ball with a strip of the cut egg, blanched mitsuba, or sliced crab stick to create a band. Repeat with the remaining ingredients.

6. In a small bowl, combine all the ingredients for the mustard soy sauce. Serve alongside the rice balls.

Tomato Stuffed Rice Balls

This show-stopping rice ball has stir-fried rice snugly packed into a hollowed-out tomato.

Ingredients

8 small tomatoes

2 tablespoons neutral oil

½ green bell pepper, finely chopped

½ red bell pepper, finely chopped

⅓ yellow bell pepper, finely chopped

⅓ zucchini, finely chopped

parsley, finely chopped, to taste

4 cups warm rice

pinch of salt

1 slice American cheese, cut into thin strips

Directions

1. Prepare the tomatoes by cutting off the stem ends and carefully hollowing out using a small spoon. Reserve the stem tops.

2. Heat the cooking oil in a large pan over medium heat, then stir-fry the chopped vegetables until slightly tender before adding the rice, stirring until golden, and seasoning with salt.

3. Preheat the oven to 400°F. Place the hollowed-out tomatoes on a sheet pan. Fill with the stir-fried rice and top each with thinly sliced cheese arranged in a cross pattern. Bake in the oven for approximately 10 minutes; you can also microwave on high for about 1 minute.

4. Cover each tomato with its stem end, then wrap each tomato individually in plastic wrap for packing, or serve directly on a plate without covering.

Anchovy Rice Balls

Fried anchovies nestled in tangy-sweet rice are a flavorful, calcium-rich snack.

Ingredients

¼ cup small dried anchovies

2 tablespoons cooking oil, divided

4 cups seasoned rice (see page 3)

¼ cup finely chopped parsley

Anchovy Seasoning

2 teaspoons gochujang

½ tablespoon soy sauce

½ teaspoon minced fresh garlic

1 tablespoon rice wine (cheongju)

Directions

1. Put the anchovies into a colander and gently shake, allowing broken bits and small pieces to fall through.

2. Heat a tablespoon of oil in a medium frying pan over medium-high heat, then stir-fry the dried anchovies until golden brown. This helps remove the fishy taste. Remove from heat and wipe out the pan.

3. Heat the remaining oil over medium-high heat. Add the gochujang, soy sauce, and minced garlic. Stir and bring to a boil. Once bubbles start to form around the edges, add the anchovies and rice wine, quickly stir-frying them.

4. Transfer the stir-fried anchovies to a large plate to cool slightly.

5. Shape the rice into bite-size balls. With damp hands, create a well in the center of each ball and fill with seasoned anchovies. Cover with more rice and roll into balls once again.

6. Roll each rice ball lightly in the chopped parsley to coat it.

2   5   6

Stuffed Tofu Skins

These rice-stuffed tofu skins, or yubuchobap, are delicious and easy to make.

Ingredients

20 pieces inari pockets (fried tofu skins)

8 inches burdock root, peeled and cut into long pieces

1 tablespoon cooking oil

½ medium carrot, finely chopped

pinch of salt

4 cups seasoned rice (see page 3)

½ tablespoon black sesame seeds

½ tablespoon white sesame seeds

Burdock Seasoning

2 tablespoons soy sauce

1 tablespoon sugar

2 tablespoons rice wine (cheongju)

½ tablespoon neutral oil

½ tablespoon sesame oil

⅓ cup water

Directions

1. Prepare a large pot of boiling water. Blanch the inari pockets in the boiling water for a moment to remove excess oil. Drain and cool then cut the pockets diagonally in half.

2. In a medium pot of boiling water, blanch the burdock about 2 minutes or to desired tenderness. In a saucepan on medium heat, simmer the blanched burdock with the burdock seasoning until reduced and shiny, 7 to 8 minutes. Cool and dice the burdock into small pieces.

3. In a medium pan on medium-high heat, heat the cooking oil and add the chopped carrot, chopped burdock root, and salt. Cook until slightly tender. Set aside.

4. Using the same pan, lightly cook the inari pockets. Remove from the heat and let cool slightly.

5. In a large bowl, add the seasoned rice, sesame seeds, and carrot-burdock and mix well.

6. Tightly pack the rice into the inari pockets.

Curry Fried Rice Balls

This round and flat rice ball
is seasoned with various
vegetables and fragrant curry.

Ingredients

5 tablespoons cooking oil, divided

3½ ounces beef, finely chopped

1 large russet potato, peeled and finely chopped

½ large carrot, peeled and finely chopped

3 cups warm rice

pinch of salt

¼ cup curry powder

½ cup all-purpose flour

2 eggs

Directions

1. Heat 2 tablespoons of the oil in a medium pan on medium-high heat and stir-fry the beef until cooked.

2. Add the potato and carrot until cooked through. And rice and combine well. Season with salt to taste.

3. Add the curry powder and continue to stir-fry until everything is evenly coated.

4. Remove from heat and allow the cooked rice to cool slightly. Once cool enough to handle, form into round, flat balls.

5. Heat the remaining 3 tablespoons of oil in a large frying pan on medium heat. Lightly sprinkle the rice balls with flour.

6. Beat the eggs in a medium bowl. One by one, dip the floured rice balls into the egg batter and fry on both sides until golden brown.

2   3   6

Curry Rice Balls

Calling all curry lovers! If you want to make these aromatic rice balls even more perfect, get some round sushi molds to form flawless spheres.

Ingredients

½ tablespoon cooking oil

7 ounces cooked ham, finely chopped

⅓ medium zucchini, finely chopped

½ large yellow onion, finely chopped

⅓ large carrot, finely chopped

4 cups warm rice

Curry Seasoning

5 tablespoons curry powder

splash of sesame oil

pinch of salt

black pepper powder, to taste

Sauce

3 tablespoons ketchup

2 tablespoons barbecue sauce

Directions

1. In a large frying pan over medium heat, heat the oil. Add the ham and vegetables and stir-fry until the vegetables are tender.

2. Add the rice and curry powder to the pan and stir-fry until well combined. Season with sesame oil, salt, and black pepper powder to taste. Remove from heat and allow to cool.

3. Place a bite-size amount of the rice mixture in plastic wrap and shape into a ball. Repeat with the remaining rice.

4. Combine the sauce ingredients in a small bowl. Drizzle on top of the rice balls before serving.

Tuna Rice Balls

Topped with grilled tuna and vegetables, this refreshing rice ball is perfect for a yummy and nutritious to-go lunch.

Ingredients

½ pound frozen sushi-grade tuna, cut into 1-inch-thick rectangular planks

pinch of coarse salt

1 egg yolk

⅓ cup sesame seeds

3 tablespoons cooking oil

4 cups seasoned rice (see page 3)

Pickled Topping

1 tablespoon rice vinegar

1 tablespoon sugar

pinch of salt

¼ cup thinly sliced daikon radish, preferably the Korean variety

¼ cup beet, thinly sliced

¼ onion, thinly sliced

Mustard Soy Sauce

2 tablespoons soy sauce

2 teaspoons mild mustard

Directions

1. Soak the tuna pieces in lukewarm water with coarse salt and let them thaw halfway. Drain and wrap in paper towels, then put in the refrigerator until completely thawed.

3. Make the pickled topping. In a medium bowl, combine the vinegar, sugar, and salt. Soak the radish, beets, and onion in a bowl of cold water. Drain and add to the vingear and sugar mixture.

4. In a small bowl, whisk the egg yolk. Using a pastry brush, coat the pieces of tuna with the yolk.

5. Spread the sesame seeds on a plate. Coat the tuna pieces in sesame seeds.

6. Heat a large pan over medium-high heat. Add enough cooking oil to coat the pan. Once hot, place the tuna pieces in the pan and cook. Flip occasionally until they are lightly browned on both sides and slightly cooked through. Slice the tuna into ¼-inch-thick pieces.

7. Tightly pack the seasoned rice into a square pan lined in plastic wrap to form a flat square shape.

8. Lift the rice out of the container using the plastic wrap, and place on a cutting board. Remove the wrap, then cut into bite-size pieces. Place a tuna steak on top of each piece of rice, then add the radish, beet, and onion pickles.

9. In a small bowl, combine the ingredients for the mustard soy sauce. Serve alongside the rice balls.

Ssambap

Furikake-seasoned rice wrapped
in various leafy greens creates
a wonderfully crunchy and
health-conscious rice ball.

Ingredients

4 cups seasoned rice (see page 3)

25 to 30 leaves of various leafy greens like Romaine, raddichio, cabbage, perilla, shiso, or kelp, trimmed to equal size, for wrapping

Rice Seasoning

2 tablespoons sesame oil

2 tablespoons sesame seeds

1 tablespoon furikake

salt, to taste

Ssamjang

6 tablespoons gochujang

¼ cup ground beef

½ tablespoon sesame oil

1 teaspoon minced fresh garlic

2 teaspoons rice wine (cheongju)

salt and pepper, to taste

Directions

1. In a large bowl, add the seasoned rice, sesame oil, sesame seeds, furikake, and salt. Mix well.

2. If using kelp, rinse thoroughly to remove excess salt and soak in cold water until sufficiently softened before trimming.

3. Combine all the ssamjang ingredients in a deep pan, and fry until fragrant. Remove from the heat.

4. Place a spoonful of seasoned rice on each leaf, then top with the stir-fried ssamjang. Roll and serve.

Furikake Rice Balls

Simple and delicious, this easy-to-make rice ball lets you get creative with fun shapes and sizes. You can also crush seasoned seaweed flakes or add stir-fried kimchi inside the rice before shaping if you want to add more flavor.

Ingredients

4 cups warm rice

4 tablespoons furikake (or seasoned seaweed flakes)

sesame oil, to taste

Directions

1. Add the freshly cooked rice to a large bowl and mix to release the steam to avoid soggy rice. While it's still warm, sprinkle furikake evenly over the rice and mix well.

2. Drizzle a few drops of sesame oil over the rice and gently mix.

3. Use a rice mold to shape the rice into balls, or simply use your hands to firmly press and shape the rice into balls. You can apply a little sesame oil to your hands to prevent sticking.

Yakbap Rice Balls

Yakbap (also called yaksik) is a glutinous rice cake that's steamed with brown sugar, sesame oil, jujube, and chestnuts. Wrapping rice in leafy greens makes it easy to eat and digest, and perfect for packing in lunch boxes.

Ingredients

3 cups glutinous rice

10 chestnuts, peeled and halved

5 dried jujubes, deseeded and halved

8 mustard green leaves or another broad leafy green

Rice Seasoning

3 tablespoons soy sauce

4 tablespoons brown sugar

1 tablespoon sesame oil

salt, to taste

Leaf Seasoning

2 teaspoons sesame oil

salt, to taste

Dipping Sauce

3 tablespoons soy sauce

1 tablespoon sesame oil

1 teaspoon minced fresh garlic

1 teaspoon sesame seeds

½ teaspoon red pepper flakes

Directions

1. Soak the glutinous rice in water for about 30 minutes, then drain.

2. To make the rice, put the soaked glutinous rice in a pressure cooker along with the chestnuts, jujubes, and all of the rice seasoning ingredients. Add slightly less water than usual and cook the rice.

3. If using mustard greens, blanch before using. Rinse and dry mustard greens or leafy green leaves. In a large bowl, marinate leaves with sesame oil and salt.

4. When rice is done cooking, put in a large wide dish and let cool slightly. Wrap a spoonful of rice mixture in each leaf. Arrange the wrapped rice on a plate.

5. Combine all the ingredients for the dipping sauce in a small bowl. Serve the rice balls with the dipping sauce.

Bulgogi Rice Balls

These rice balls make for a full meal, with each bite containing both rice and meat. Parsley in the rice seasoning adds a bit of freshness to the combination.

Ingredients

⅔ pound beef brisket

5 cloves garlic, thinly sliced

1 tablespoon cooking oil

4 cups warm rice

1 tablespoon finely minced minari (Chinese celery) or watercress

salt, to taste

Beef Seasoning

3 tablespoons neutral oil

2 tablespoons soy sauce

1 tablespoon sesame oil

salt and pepper, to taste

Directions

1. Prep the beef by gently pounding with the back of a knife before thinly slicing.

2. In a large pan or skillet on medium-high heat, add all the ingredients for the beef seasoning and bring to a boil. Add the beef and sliced garlic, flipping until they are evenly cooked. Remove from heat. Cut the cooked beef into bite-size square pieces and set aside with the cooked sliced garlic.

3. In another large pan or skillet, heat the cooking oil over medium heat. Add the rice and minari, stir-frying until lightly browned. Remove from heat and season with salt.

4. Shape the fried rice in rectangular, bite-size portions. Top with a square of the cooked beef and a slice of cooked garlic.

Kimchi Fried Rice Pancakes

Finely chopped kimchi, Spam, bell peppers, mozzarella, and rice make up the batter for this delicious pan-fried pancake. This one is a particular winner with children!

Ingredients

3 cups warm rice

9 ounces cabbage kimchi, drained and chopped to ¼-inch strips

¼ onion, chopped to ¼-inch pieces

¼ green bell pepper, chopped to ¼-inch pieces

¼ red bell pepper, chopped to ¼-inch pieces

1 (12-ounce) can Spam, cut into ¼-inch cubes

4 eggs

½ cup flour

8 ounces mozzarella

cooking oil, as needed

Directions

1. To make the batter, combine the rice, chopped kimchi, onion, bell peppers, Spam, eggs, and flour in a large bowl. Add mozzerella cheese and mix until just combined.

2. In a large pan, heat enough cooking oil to coat the pan generously over medium heat. Spoon ¼ cup of the batter into the pan, shaping into a round flat shape. Cook until both sides are golden brown. Repeat with the remaining batter.

MASTERING THE BASICS OF ROLLS

Making Rolls Neatly

Spreading Rice. Spreading the sushi rice beyond the seaweed sheet's surface will create a cleaner look because only the seaweed will be visible when rolled.

Order of Ingredients. If using mustard or cream cheese, spread them first. Arrange easily scattered ingredients like sliced vegetables or roe neatly before larger ingredients. Pay attention to the order of placing the ingredients to ensure a nice mix of colors.

Wrapping with a Sushi Mat. The sushi mat is an essential tool for making rolls and should not be omitted. Wrap the sushi mat entirely in plastic wrap to prevent the rice from sticking to the mat or your hands.

Wetting Hands with Water. When rolling with dry hands, rice grains tend to stick everywhere. Wet your hands thoroughly with water mixed with a few drops of lemon juice or vinegar to avoid sticking.

Spreading and Flipping Rice. Place the seaweed on the wrapped sushi mat, spread the rice evenly, and then flip it over so that the rice side faces down and the seaweed side faces up.

Roll from the Bottom. Grab the sushi mat and roll it upward, pulling toward yourself while rolling forward. Applying a slight pressure at the fingertips while rolling helps maintain the shape.

Slice with a Wet Knife. If you're not confident in slicing cleanly, you can slice the roll while it's wrapped in plastic wrap to prevent it from falling apart. However, be careful not to let the sliced plastic wrap pieces get inside. Wetting the knife before slicing can help. When slicing, avoid pressing down all at once and instead slice back and forth in a sawing motion.

Five Basic Styles of Rolls

California Roll. The California roll is the most basic type of roll, characterized by rice that is visible on the outside. It's also called "naked sushi." Depending on the ingredients inside, the nature of the roll can vary. Typically, a California roll includes avocado, crab meat, and roe.

Sushi Roll. Sushi rolls, unlike California rolls, are topped with various types of raw fish or seafood, or include raw fish cut inside the roll. When placing raw fish on the surface of the roll, you can either use one type or arrange multiple types of raw fish for a colorful presentation.

Tempura Roll. Tempura is a common Japanese fried food. Tempura can be inside the roll or placed on top, providing a crispy texture. Japanese-style tempura used in rolls is typically thinly coated and crispier compared to other tempura. Tempura used in roll recipes usually includes shrimp, squid, or mussels. Sometimes, tonkatsu (fried pork cutlet) is added, or the entire roll is coated in tempura batter and fried.

Cream Cheese Roll. These rolls are filled with cream cheese, providing a rich and deep flavor. Most rolls with cream cheese also contain smoked salmon because no other fish complements cream cheese as well.

Grilled Sauce Roll. After applying a unique sauce to the roll, grill or bake it. Although the method of making the sauce varies, it's usually made by mixing mayonnaise with chili sauce, hot sauce, and roe.

Grilled sauce rolls typically use the basic California roll with ingredients such as avocado, crab meat, and cucumber. After the roll is completed and sliced, additional ingredients such as salmon, tuna, or crab meat can be added, and then the sauce is applied and baked in the oven.

Art in a single bite!

Part 3 Rice Rolls

Rice rolls can combine fresh fish, various vegetables, fruits, and even cheese to make not only visually appealing but also delicious snacks or meals. While making sushi rolls may seem difficult, they are actually easy and redundant once you know how.

Avocado Crab Roll

Inspired by the California roll, this roll contains imitation crab meat and roe. Topped with avocado, it is smooth and savory.

Ingredients

4 tablespoons flying fish roe

4 crab sticks, torn into thin strips

4 sheets roasted seaweed

4 cups seasoned rice (see page 3)

1 cucumber, thinly sliced with skin on

½ avocado, thinly sliced lengthwise

Yogurt Sauce

3 tablespoons plain yogurt

2 tablespoons mayonnaise

Directions

1. Rinse the flying fish roe under running water in a strainer. Drain well.

2. In medium bowl, mix the ingredients for the yogurt sauce. Add the crab sticks and flying fish roe and mix well.

3. Cut the seaweed sheets to the size of the sushi mat

4. Place a seaweed sheet on a mat wrapped in plastic wrap. Spread a layer of the rice evenly over the sheet. Flip the sheet over so that the rice is on the bottom and the seaweed is on the top.

5. Place a row of sliced cucumber topped with the yogurt-crab mixture on the seaweed. Using the sushi mat, press firmly and roll tightly.

6. Place the sliced avocado on top of the roll and wrap tightly with plastic wrap, gently pressing to ensure the avocado sticks to the roll.

7. Place the plastic-wrapped roll on a cutting board, cut into bite-size pieces with care so that the avocado does not spread, then remove the plastic wrap. Repeat steps 4 to 7 with the remaining ingredients.

Salmon Roll

A delicious salmon roll made with smoked salmon and cream cheese, paired with a tangy mustard sauce.

Ingredients

4 sheets roasted seaweed

4 cups seasoned rice (see page 3)

8 ounces smoked salmon slices, divided into 6 portions

1 (3-ounce) pack alfalfa sprouts

½ (8-ounce) package cream cheese, softened

Wasabi Sauce

2 tablespoons wasabi

3 tablespoons mayonnaise

1 teaspoon sugar

Directions

1. In a small bowl, combine all ingredients for the wasabi sauce.

2. Cut the seaweed sheets to the size of the sushi mat.

3. Place a seaweed sheet on a mat wrapped in plastic wrap. Spread a layer of the rice evenly over the sheet. Flip the sheet over so that the rice is on the bottom and the seaweed is on the top.

4. Place half a slice of smoked salmon, some alfalfa sprouts, and 1 tablespoon cream cheese on top of the seaweed. Using the sushi mat, press firmly and roll tightly.

5. Place the other half of the smoked salmon slice on top of the roll, then wrap tightly with plastic wrap and lightly press to shape it.

6. Slice the roll into bite-size pieces with the plastic wrap still on to prevent from falling apart, then remove the wrap and serve on a plate. Repeat steps 3 to 6 with the remaining seaweed sheets and ingredients.

Cream Cheese Roll

This is a roll with a rich and deep flavor, thanks to the addition of cream cheese. Pair with a glass of rosé or white wine.

Ingredients

4 sheets roasted seaweed

4 cups seasoned rice (see page 3)

½ (8-ounce) package cream cheese, cold, cut into finger-size strips

½ avocado, thickly sliced lengthwise

3 red cabbage leaves, thinly sliced

Directions

1. Cut the seaweed sheets to the size of the sushi mat.

2. Spread a thin layer of rice over a seaweed sheet. Turn the sheet over so that the seaweed faces up and the rice faces down.

3. Place 2 to 3 strips of cream cheese, avocado, and red cabbage on the seaweed sheet, then roll tightly using the sushi mat.

4. Cut the roll into bite-size pieces and arrange them neatly on a plate. Repeat the steps with the remaining seaweed sheets and ingredients.

Steak Roll

A soft sirloin steak flavored with deli sauce fills this roll. The combination of crunchy cucumber, onion, and melting steak in your mouth is excellent.

Ingredients

½ pound beef sirloin, cut into finger-thick slices

salt and pepper, to taste

4 sheets roasted seaweed

4 cups seasoned rice (see page 3)

½ onion, thinly sliced and rinsed to remove some of the pungent flavor

½ cucumber, thinly sliced

¼ cup mixed greens

Deli Sauce

4 tablespoons steak sauce

2 tablespoons teriyaki sauce

2 tablespoons red wine vinegar

Directions

1. Season the beef with salt and pepper. Grill lightly on a grill or pan to desired doneness.

2. Put all the ingredients for the deli sauce in a small saucepan and bring to a boil. Remove from heat.

3. Place the cooked sirloin into the sauce. Make sure the steak is fully coated in sauce.

4. Cut the seaweed sheets to the size of the sushi mat.

5. Spread a thin layer of rice over a seaweed sheet. Turn the sheet over so that the seaweed faces up and the rice faces down.

6. Place the sirloin, onion, and cucumber on the sheet then drizzle with the deli sauce. Roll firmly with the sushi mat.

7. Place the rolled-up roll on a cutting board, press lightly with your palm, then cut into bite-size pieces. Top with baby greens and more deli sauce. Repeat step 5 with the remaining seaweed sheets and ingredients.

Crunchy Shrimp Roll

A crispy and savory shrimp tempura fills this roll. The crunchy bread crumb topping adds a crispy texture as well as a decorative touch!

Ingredients

8 large shrimp, shelled and deveined with tails intact

2 cups neutral oil

4 sheets roasted seaweed

4 cups seasoned rice (see page 3)

1 cucumber, deseeded, julienned, and ends cut

Batter

½ cup packaged tempura frying powder

½ cup ice water

Sauce

3 tablespoons mayonnaise

1 tablespoon Japanese hot mustard (karashi)

2 tablespoons peanuts, shelled and finely chopped

1 tablespoon dried parsley

Directions

1. Rinse the shelled shrimp in lightly salted water, then pat dry with paper towels.

2. Place the oil in a large pan over high heat. In a large bowl, combine the batter ingredients. One at a time, coat the shrimp with tempura batter and fry until golden and crispy.

3. Once the shrimp is cooked, pour the remaining tempura batter into the hot oil. Fry briefly to make tempura flakes for topping.

4. In a small bowl, combine the sauce ingredients.

5. Cut the seaweed sheets to the size of the sushi mat.

6. Spread a thin layer of rice over a seaweed sheet. Turn the sheet over so that the seaweed faces up. Place 2 to 3 fried shrimp, some sliced cucumber, tempura flakes, and sauce on the seaweed. Roll up tightly with the sushi mat.

7. Cut into bite-size pieces and serve with the remaining tempura and sauce. Repeat steps 6 and 7 with the remaining seaweed sheets and ingredients.

2

3

4

6

Spicy Tuna Roll

This spicy roll is made with tuna marinated in a mixture of gochujang, gochugaru, and mustard.

Ingredients

10 to 11 ounces frozen sushi-grade tuna steak

salt, to taste

1/3 cup flying fish roe

1/4 red onion, thinly sliced

4 sheets roasted seaweed

4 cups seasoned rice (see page 3)

Spicy Sauce

3 tablespoons wasabi

4 tablespoons mayonnaise

2 tablespoons cream cheese

1 teaspoon gochujang

1 tablespoon gochugaru, cayenne, or finely minced jalapeño

2 teaspoons corn syrup

Directions

1. Thaw the frozen tuna in a 3% saltwater solution (1 ounce of salt per quart) for about 30 seconds. Remove from the saltwater and roughly chop. Place in a medium mixing bowl.

2. Lightly rinse the flying fish roe in a strainer. Drain well. Add to the bowl with the prepared tuna.

3. Rinse the red onion slices in water to remove some of the raw onion's pungent flavor.

4. In a small bowl, combine all the ingredients for the spicy sauce. Add 3/4 of the prepared sauce into the bowl with the prepared tuna and flying fish roe.

5. Cut the seaweed sheets to the size of the sushi mat.

6. Spread a thin layer of rice over a seaweed sheet. Turn the sheet over so that the seaweed faces up. Add about 1/6 of the tuna and roe mixture down the center of the sheet. Roll up tightly with the sushi mat.

7. Place the sliced onion on top of the rolled sushi, then cut into bite-size pieces and sprinkle the remaining sauce. Repeat with the remaining seaweed sheets and ingredients.

Radish Wrap Roll

Seasoned radish wrap gives this roll a sweet and sour flavor, with a satisfying crunch from the cucumber and carrot.

Ingredients

1 cucumber, cut lengthwise into thin, ¼-inch-thick strips

½ large carrot, peeled and julienned

1 package fried tofu pockets (about 8 pockets)

18 radish wraps

red food coloring or beet juice mixed with water

yellow food coloring or ground mustard mixed with water

splash of cooking oil

salt, to taste

4 cups seasoned rice (see page 3)

Directions

1. Sprinkle the cucumber strips with a little salt and let sit for 10 to 15 minutes. Pat dry with a paper towel to remove excess moisture.

2. In a medium frying pan or skillet over medium heat, add a small amount of oil. Once hot, add the sliced carrot and sauté until slightly softened, stirring occasionally, about 5 to 7 minutes. Squeeze the excess liquid out of the tofu pockets. Slice to ¼-inch strips.

3. Soak 6 sheets of radish wrap in red food coloring/beet water to turn them red, and soak another 6 sheets in yellow food coloring/mustard water to turn them yellow. Leave 6 sheets of radish wrap as they are (white).

4. Cover a sushi roller with plastic wrap. Overlap the radish wraps halfway, alternating the white, yellow, and red ones. Spread the seasoned rice over them, add the cucumber, carrot, and tofu skin, then tightly roll up using the sushi roller. Slice into bite-size pieces. Repeat with the remaining ingredients.

Part 4 Sandwiches

A sandwich offers not only convenience and speed but also tons of flavor and nourishment. Sandwiches are the ideal choice for a quick breakfast, a special item in lunch or picnic baskets, or a nutritious snack for children and adults alike!

Club Sandwiches

This hearty chicken club is paired with a generous serving of mustard sauce for a zesty kick!

Ingredients

8 slices white bread

4 tablespoons butter

4 chicken breasts

salt and pepper, to taste

1 tablespoon cooking oil

8 lettuce leaves

4 slices cheddar cheese

½ onion, sliced into rings and rinsed to remove pungent flavor

1 large tomato, sliced into rings

4 tablespoons yellow mustard

¼ cup grated Parmesan cheese

Directions

1. Lightly toast the bread slices in a warm pan or toaster. Once cooled to room temperature, spread with butter.

2. Flatten the chicken breast by gently pressing with the flat side of a knife. Make small cuts on both sides and sprinkle with salt and pepper. In a medium pan over medium heat, add the cooking oil. Once hot, cook the seasoned chicken, flipping to cook evenly on both sides.

3. Assemble the sandwich. On a slice of bread, lay a piece of lettuce, cheddar cheese, onion, tomato, and chicken breast. Generously drizzle mustard and sprinkle a little grated Parmesan cheese. Top with another piece of lettuce and cover with another slice of bread. Repeat with the remaining ingredients to make a total of 4 sandwiches.

Steak Sandwiches

This sandwich perfectly combines the flavors of beef seasoned with a rich steak sauce and sautéed mushrooms.

Ingredients

8 slices white bread

4 tablespoons butter

14 ounces sirloin steak

2 tablespoons cooking oil, divided

6 button mushrooms, thinly sliced

1 onion, thinly sliced

8 lettuce leaves

1 tomato, sliced into rings

finely chopped fresh parsley, to taste

mayonnaise, to taste (optional)

Beef Marinade

3 tablespoons red wine

salt and pepper, to taste

Directions

1. Lightly toast the bread slices in a warm pan or toaster. Spread butter on each slice.

2. Prepare the beef tenderloin, slicing it slightly thinner than a regular steak. Combine the ingredients for the beef marinade in a shallow bowl, then add the steak to marinate.

3. In a medium pan or skillet on medium-high heat, add 1 tablespoon of the cooking oil. Once hot, cook the beef, flipping to cook evenly on both sides to desired rareness. During cooking, drizzle steak sauce for a rich flavor.

4. In another medium pan, sauté the mushrooms and onion over medium heat with the remaining tablespoon of oil. Season with salt to taste.

5. Assemble the sandwich. Place two lettuce leaves on a slice of bread, followed by the cooked steak, sautéed mushrooms and onions, tomato, and parsley. Cover with another slice of bread. You can try adding a little mayonnaise for extra flavor. Repeat with the remaining ingredients to make a total of 4 sandwiches.

Tricolor Sandwiches

A basic sandwich where finely chopped cucumbers and carrots are mixed in mashed potatoes and creamy mayonnaise and placed between slices of bread.

Ingredients

12 slices white bread

4 tablespoons butter

2 medium cucumbers, finely chopped

1 large carrot, finely chopped

3 medium potatoes, peeled and cut into large pieces

½ cup mayonnaise

8 slices cheddar cheese

salt and pepper, to taste

Directions

1. Lightly toast the bread slices then spread butter on each slice.

2. Place the cucumbers and carrots in separate medium bowls lined with paper towels. Add a pinch of salt to each, and let sit for about 10 minutes. Then squeeze out the excess moisture.

3. Boil the potatoes in a pot of water with a pinch of salt until they are tender. Drain the water and mash.

4. Combine the drained cucumbers and carrots with ⅓ of the mayonnaise each. Mix the mashed potatoes with ⅓ of the mayonnaise and add a little pepper. Mix everything thoroughly.

5. Assemble the sandwich: On one slice of bread, place a slice of cheddar cheese, followed by the cucumber mixture. Place another slice of bread on top and add a slice of cheddar cheese and the mashed potatoes. Top with another slice of bread and add the carrot mixture. Finally, cover with another slice of bread.

6. Cut into halves: Press the sandwich with something heavy to compress the layers. Once it settles, trim the edges and cut into half. Repeat steps 5 to 6 with the remaining bread slices and ingredients.

Ham and Egg Sandwiches

This nutritious classic is filled with cooked ham, boiled eggs, and vegetables. Pair it with a glass of milk for a well-balanced meal.

Ingredients

8 slices white bread

4 tablespoons butter

5 large eggs

1 teaspoon cooking oil

4 slices deli ham

8 leaves Romaine lettuce

½ yellow onion, sliced into rings and rinsed to remove pungent flavor

4 tablespoons ketchup

3 tablespoons mayonnaise

salt and pepper, to taste

Directions

1. Toast the bread slices until they are crispy. Spread butter on each slice.

2. In a saucepan or pot large enough to fit all the eggs, add all 5 eggs and cover with water. Bring to a boil. Once boiling, cover and remove from heat. After 12 minutes, put the eggs in a bowl filled with ice water. Once cool, peel and thickly slice.

3. In a medium pan over medium heat, add the cooking oil. Once the oil is hot, cook the ham slices until crispy. Place on a paper towel to remove excess grease.

4. Assemble the sandwich. Place the sliced eggs on one slice of bread and sprinkle with a pinch of salt and pepper. On top of the eggs, add the ham, Romaine lettuce, and onion rings. Drizzle with ketchup and mayonnaise. Finally, cover with another slice of bread and cut the sandwich to your desired size for serving. Repeat with the remaining ingredients to make a total of 4 sandwiches.

Pancake Sandwiches

Create a homemade version of
a Korean street food classic.

Ingredients

8 slices white bread

4 large eggs

¼ small cabbage, finely shredded with a box grater

1 small carrot, finely shredded with a box grater

salt, to taste

pinch of sugar, plus more to taste

¼ cup butter

4 tablespoons ketchup

Directions

1. Toast the bread slices until they turn golden brown on both sides.

2. In a large bowl, beat the eggs until well mixed. Add the shredded cabbage and carrot to the beaten eggs, and season the mixture with a pinch of salt and sugar to taste. Mix everything together thoroughly.

3. In the medium pan over medium-high heat, melt the butter. Pour about ¼ of the egg and vegetable mixture into the pan (this will be equivalent to 1 serving). Cook the mixture, flipping occasionally until it has a well-cooked, omelette-like consistency. Repeat with the remaining egg mixture.

4. Assemble the sandwich. Place 1 slice of toasted bread on a clean surface. Spread the cooked egg and vegetable filling on top of the bread. Drizzle ketchup and sprinkle sugar evenly over the filling. Place another slice of toasted bread on top to complete. Repeat with the remaining ingredients until you have 4 sandwiches.

Chicken Sliders

Spicy chicken breast and sharp,
raw onions are nestled within
a soft roll for a crowd-pleasing
sandwich your family will enjoy.

Ingredients

8 rolls, halved

6 tablespoons butter

8 chicken breast fillets, sliced into ½-inch-thick strips

salt and pepper, to taste

1 teaspoon minced fresh Italian parsley, divided

1 tablespoon cooking oil

2 tablespoons Dijon mustard

4 tablespoons yellow mustard

8 leaves Romaine lettuce

½ onion, sliced into rings, soaked, and dried to reduce spiciness

1 tomato, sliced into rings

Directions

1. Spread butter on each roll half.

2. Season the chicken breast slices with salt, pepper, and ½ teaspoon of parsley. In a medium pan over medium heat, add cooking oil. Once hot, add chicken and stir-fry until cooked through.

3. Combine the Dijon mustard and yellow mustard in a small mixing bowl.

4. Assemble the sandwich. Place 2 lettuce leaves on a roll, followed by layers of onion rings, chicken breast, and tomato. Drizzle the mixed mustard sauce over the top. Sprinkle with a bit of remaining parsley and cover with the other half of the roll, gently pressing down. Repeat with the remaining ingredients until you have 4 sandwiches total.

Chicken Teriyaki Sandwiches

This sandwich boasts teriyaki chicken tenders with fresh lettuce and generous portions of onion, delivering a savory crunch.

café

won't you talk over

a cup of drink?

Ingredients

1 to 2 tablespoons neutral cooking oil

8 slices white bread

8 chicken breasts

4 Romaine lettuce leaves, torn to size of bread

fresh chicory, leaves only (optional)

1 tomato, thinly sliced

¼ onion, thinly sliced

2 tablespoons chopped pickles

5 tablespoons grated Parmesan cheese

Teriyaki Sauce

5 tablespoons soy sauce

2 tablespoons olive oil

4 cloves garlic

1 dried red pepper

2 lemon slices

1 tablespoon sesame oil

2 teaspoon sugar

¼ cup water

salt and pepper, to taste

Directions

1. Toast the bread slices in a warm pan or toaster until crisp.

2. In a medium saucepan over medium heat, combine the ingredients for the teriyaki sauce. Simmer the sauce until it reduces by half, then strain out any solids.

3. Heat the cooking oil in a medium pan over low heat. Add the chicken breast to the pan and cook over low heat until partially cooked. Once the chicken is partially cooked, add about a third of the teriyaki sauce to the pan and continue cooking until the chicken is fully cooked and the sauce has coated the chicken evenly.

4. Assemble the sandwich. On a slice of toasted bread, arrange a layer of Romaine lettuce and chicory, followed by slices of tomato and onion. Place the grilled chicken breast on top and sprinkle with chopped pickles and Parmesan cheese. Drizzle the remaining teriyaki sauce over the ingredients. Top with another slice of toasted bread and press gently to create the sandwich. Repeat with the remaining ingredients until you have 4 sandwiches total.

Smoked Salmon Sandwiches

This sandwich features smoked salmon topped with onions, capers, and chicory for a refreshing and lively flavor.

Ingredients

8 slices whole-grain bread

5 tablespoons mayonnaise

12 slices smoked salmon

½ onion, finely chopped

3 tablespoons capers, drained and rinsed

handful of fresh chicory or frisée

pepper, to taste

Cream Sauce

4 tablespoons mayonnaise

2 tablespoons heavy cream

salt and pepper, to taste

Directions

1. Lightly toast the bread slices in a warm pan or toaster until golden brown, then generously spread mayonnaise on each slice of bread.

2. Place the smoked salmon on a paper towel and pat dry. Sprinkle a pinch of black pepper over the smoked salmon to season.

3. In a medium mixing bowl, combine the mayonnaise and heavy cream for the cream sauce. Mix well. Season with salt and pepper to taste.

4. Assemble the sandwich. Lay three slices of smoked salmon on the bread, folding them if necessary to fit the slices. Sprinkle the chopped onion and capers over the salmon. Add the chicory or frisee on top. Generously drizzle the cream sauce over the greens. Place another slice of bread on top to complete the sandwich. Repeat with the remaining ingredients.

Apple Cinnamon Toast

This sweet treat features caramelized apples with a hint of cinnamon on toasted bread. It pairs perfectly with a cup of coffee.

Ingredients

8 slices white bread

3½ tablespoons butter

4 red apples, any type, cored, halved, and sliced into half-moons

6 tablespoons brown sugar

4 tablespoons ground cinnamon

Directions

1. Toast the bread slices in a warm pan or toaster until crisp.

2. Grease a medium pan with butter and set to medium heat. Arrange the sliced apples in a single layer and sprinkle the brown sugar evenly on top. Cook the apples for about 20 minutes, turning them infrequently so they become golden and caramelized.

3. Sprinkle the cinnamon lightly over the apples. Continue cooking for an additional 10 minutes, until the apples are tender and infused with the cinnamon flavor.

4. Place ¼ of the caramelized apple mixture onto one slice of the toasted bread. Cover with another slice of bread to create a sandwich. Repeat with the remaining ingredients.

Brie Bagel Sandwiches

This sandwich combines Brie, apples, and a nutty honey sauce.

Ingredients

8 ounces Brie, sliced

1 apple, thinly sliced

4 bagels, halved

handful of fresh dill

Peanut Honey Sauce

¼ cup crushed or chopped peanuts

6 tablespoons honey

Directions

1. In a small bowl, mix the crushed peanuts with honey until well combined.

2. Arrange the cheese and sliced apple neatly on the bagel halves. Generously spread the peanut honey sauce in an even layer over the ingredients. Finally, add the dill and place the other half of the bagel on top to complete the sandwich. Repeat with the remaining ingredients.

Hot Dog Sandwiches

This sandwich features savory hot dogs that pair perfectly with the substantial baguette.

Ingredients

4 mini baguettes (or hot dog buns), sliced lengthwise

5 tablespoons butter

4 hot dogs

1 onion, sliced

8 Romaine lettuce leaves

6 dill pickles, sliced lengthwise and dried

8 tablespoons ketchup

1 tablespoon neutral cooking oil, divided

salt and pepper, to taste

Directions

1. Spread the butter on the baguette slices. Toast the buttered baguette halves in a medium pan on low heat until slightly crispy.

2. Prep the hot dogs by making 2 to 3 shallow cuts on each, then sprinkling with salt and pepper to taste. Heat 1½ tablespoons cooking oil in a medium pan on medium heat, add the hot dogs, and cook until browned. Remove from heat and cut each hot dog in half lengthwise.

3. Heat the remaining cooking oil in a medium pan over medium heat then sauté the onion with salt and pepper until tender.

4. To assemble the sandwich, place two leaves of Romaine lettuce on a baguette half. Layer on the sautéed onions, dill pickles, and one hot dog. Sprinkle a bit more pepper and generously top with ketchup. Finally, cover with the other half of the baguette and press gently. Repeat with the remaining ingredients.

Tuna Croissant Sandwiches

For a satisfying midday meal, try this filling sandwich with tuna salad heaped on a crisp and soft croissant.

Ingredients

4 croissants, halved lengthwise

4 tablespoons butter

2 (5-ounce) cans tuna

1 bunch fresh dill

4 lettuce leaves or 1 cup fresh chicory (optional)

Salad Dressing

½ green bell pepper, finely diced

½ red bell pepper, finely diced

3 pickles, finely diced

¼ onion, finely diced

4 tablespoons mayonnaise

salt and pepper, to taste

Directions

1. Evenly spread the butter on each croissant half.

2. Drain the canned tuna with a strainer, removing excess oil. Transfer to a large bowl.

3. In the large bowl, combine the drained tuna with the diced bell peppers, pickles, onions, mayonnaise, salt, and pepper. Mix everything well until evenly blended.

4. Assemble the sandwiches by filling the croissants with the tuna salad mixture and a sprig of dill on top. Top with the other half of the croissants to complete the sandwiches. You can also add lettuce or chicory for extra flavor and freshness.

Bulgogi Salsa Wraps

Salsa and jalapeños bring a decidedly Mexican flair to bulgogi that's enveloped in a flour tortilla. Spicy yet refreshing!

Ingredients

¾ pound beef, sliced in ¼-inch-thick pieces

cooking oil, as needed

5 tablespoons prepared salsa

8 lettuce leaves

8 large flour tortillas

1 cup sliced jalapeños (optional)

Beef Marinade

1 tablespoon sesame oil

1 teaspoon minced fresh garlic

1 teaspoon sugar

½ tablespoon rice wine (cheongju)

salt and pepper, to taste

Directions

1. In a large bowl, combine the ingredients for the beef marinade. Add the beef to the bowl.

2. Coat a large pan with oil and heat over medium heat. Stir-fry the marinated beef to desired doneness. Remove from heat.

3. Add the salsa to the cooked beef and mix thoroughly. Adjust the amount of salsa according to your desired level of spiciness.

4. Assemble the wraps. Place a lettuce leaf on each tortilla. Spoon the cooked bulgogi over the lettuce. Add the jalapeños on top, if using. Fold the tortillas in half or roll.

Salami Pizza Rolls

A creative take on pizza, this sandwich is made with a hard roll and baked to perfection.

Ingredients

8 rolls, halved

4 tablespoons butter

7 ounces salami, cut into thick slices

cooking oil, as needed

1 green bell pepper, sliced into rings

1 red bell pepper, sliced into rings

1 yellow bell pepper, sliced into rings

⅔ onion, sliced into rings

5 tablespoons green olives, chopped to small pieces

⅔ cup shredded mozzarella

Pizza Sauce

½ cup tomato sauce

1 tablespoon butter

2 teaspoons dried oregano

2 tablespoons finely chopped onion

salt and pepper, to taste

Directions

1. Preheat the oven to 400°F. Select rolls that are firm but not too hard. Spread the butter on the cut sides of the rolls and set them aside.

2. Cut the salami into thick slices. Lightly grease a medium pan with cooking oil over medium-low heat and cook the salami until slightly crispy. Remove any excess grease.

3. In a medium saucepan, combine all the pizza sauce ingredients. Heat the mixture over low heat, simmering gently for at least 10 minutes.

4. Assemble the rolls. Spread the prepared pizza sauce onto the cut sides of the rolls. Put a few slices of salami on the sauce. Add the green, red, and yellow bell peppers, onions, green olives, and mozzarella to each roll. Place the assembled rolls in the oven and bake for 5 to 8 minutes, or until the cheese has melted and the rolls are heated through. In the last 2 minutes of baking, place the other halves of the rolls on top to complete the sandwiches.

Sweet Potato Pocket Sandwiches

These pocket sandwiches are made with folded bread packed with sweet potatoes and tangy cabbage.

Ingredients

2 large sweet potatoes

1 cup heavy cream

2 cabbage leaves, finely shredded

1 medium carrot, finely shredded

2/3 cup canned corn

4 tablespoons raisins

4 tablespoons mayonnaise

8 slices white bread

Marinade

2 tablespoons rice vinegar

2 tablespoons sugar

2/3 teaspoon salt

Directions

1. Steam the sweet potatoes until they are soft. Peel the hot sweet potatoes, mash, and let cool. Then, mix in the heavy cream.

2. In a large bowl, combine the finely shredded cabbage and carrot with the marinade ingredients and marinate for about 10 minutes. Squeeze out the excess moisture. Add the drained corn, raisins, and mayonnaise to the cabbage and carrot mixture. Mix everything thoroughly.

3. On each slice of bread, spread an even layer of the prepared salad mixture, leaving a 1-centimeter border around the edges. On top of the salad mixture, spread a layer of the mashed sweet potatoes.

4. Place the prepared sandwiches in a sandwich maker or a pan with a lid and grill for about 5 minutes until they turn golden brown. Once grilled, cut the sandwiches into triangular halves.

ABOUT THE AUTHOR

Seung-Ju Choi worked as a culinary reporter for a women's lifestyle magazine for more than 10 years. Now, she is a professional chef and food stylist, catering small parties and meetings. She excels in creating easy and practical recipes for everyday Korean food, special meals, and healthy foods. In addition to *The Kimbap Cookbook*, her published books include *Today's Korean Side Dish*, *One Bowl Diet Lunch Box*, and *Pasta and Salad*. She was in charge of cooking and food styling for the Korean TV drama *Love Is Annoying, but I Don't Want to Be Lonely*.